THE
Old Photographs
SERIES

RUNCORN

Runcorn in 1870. The white building is the public salt water bath house. Behind it are Belvedere and Clarence Terrace which were built to accommodate summer visitors to pre-industrial Runcorn. Ship building and repair is taking place in the Belvedere shipyard whilst at the left of the picture the tower of the ancient windmill is visible.

THE
Old Photographs
SERIES

RUNCORN

Compiled by
Bert Starkey

CHALFORD

BATH • AUGUSTA • RENNES

First published 1994
Copyright © Bert Starkey, 1994

The Chalford Publishing Company Limited
St Mary's Mill, Chalford, Stroud
Gloucestershire GL6 8NX

ISBN 0 7524 0025 8

Typesetting & origination
by Alan Sutton Limited
Printed in Great Britain

Fishing smacks at the ferry landing about 1884.

Contents

Acknowledgements

This collection of photographs was compiled through the generosity of friends old and new. Over many years I have been given old pictures or I have been permitted to copy treasured family photographs. My thanks are due to these kind folk and I hope that my memory allows me to acknowledge my indebtedness to all of them. I would like to record my gratitude for the help afforded me by:

Mr Walter Brown, the late James Collins, Miss Josie Colley,
the late Harold Darbyshire, Mrs Ellen Dutton, Mrs Kathleen Edwards,
Mr Charles Ford, Mr Roy Gamon, Dr Patrick Greene, Mr David Griffin,
Mr Roy Gough, Mrs Julie Heron, Mrs Cynthia Hignett,
Mrs Olwen Hargreaves, Mr Arthur Houghton, Captain George Hogg RN,
Mr Peter Johnson, Mr Bill Leathwood, Miss Joan Littler, Mrs Annie London,
Mrs Margaret Locke, Miss Betty Mack, the late Alan Mack, Mr Alan Marsh,
Mrs Margaret Marsh, Mr Bob Martindale, the late Harry Naylor,
Miss Pat Nickson, Mrs Dorothy Norcross, Mr John O'Neill, Mr Jim Peden,
Mrs Dorothy Smith, Mrs Eva Stephens, Mr Aubrey Teare, Mr Peter Thomas,
Mrs Helen Worrall, Mr Keith Walker, Mrs D. Weller, Mr John Wyche,
and the staff at the Cheshire County Library, Shopping City, Runcorn.

My thanks are also due to my wife for her work in checking the manuscript and to Bill Leathwood for his help in correcting the proofs.

To David Luke.

The narrowboats 'Java' and 'Pekin' at Runcorn Docks about 1905.

Introduction

Although a Runcorn hamlet was in existence over a thousand years ago, this is a collection of images which dates from mid-Victorian times when the town was a bustling little industrial place of some seven thousand inhabitants.

At the dawn of the age of photography in the first decade of the reign of Queen Victoria, Runcorn experienced its first period of profound change. By the 1840s the town was fast losing its reputation as an attractive spa or watering place to which invalids resorted during the summer months. Besides being a shallow draught port of some consequence, the town had a number of sandstone quarries which were renowned over a wide area for the excellence of the stone they produced. The two soapworks, which had been established early in the century, had begun to manufacture their own basic chemicals and they had become the precursors of the mid-Merseyside chemical industry.

As picturesque Runcorn was transformed into a sooty industrial town, the boarding schools which had been established in Regency times for the sons and daughters of wealthy Liverpool and Manchester businessmen, began to close. In the thirty years from 1830 to 1860 the character of the town changed dramatically. When the Mersey became polluted the salt water bath house became disused and gradually atmospheric pollution from the new factories turned the red and pink sandstone of the town's churches and public buildings into a uniform black. Many of the photographs illustrate this first period of Runcorn's rapid transition from green fields to factory complex.

Mid-Victorian Runcorn was a town of streets of small cottages hemmed in between the river and the Bridgwater Canal. The town was described as 'being like the Dead Sea. There is a way into it but none out'. The photographs show how Runcorn's complete isolation was lessened with the building of the railway bridge across the Mersey in 1868 and how in 1905 the transporter bridge was built to enable vehicular traffic to cross to Widnes. The town's long period of seclusion ended with the completion of the present Mersey road bridge in 1961.

The quarries reached the zenith of their prosperity in the age of the camera but after the end of the century they began to close as the best of the stone was worked out. The photographs also record the decline of traffic on the inland waterways as business fell away in the face of competition from road and rail transport.

In 1894 Runcorn became an Urban District Council with a population of about 16,000 inhabitants and during the next half century, the town expanded to take in parts of rural Weston, Clifton and Halton. It was also in 1894 that the Manchester Ship Canal was opened and Runcorn Docks became part of the new port of Manchester. The establishment of Salt Union and the Castner-Kellner chemical works at Weston Point saw the beginning of an expansion in the local chemical industry which was to play a vital role in the nation's war effort in two World Wars.

Some of the photographs illustrate activities taking place in industries that closed many years ago. The soapworks ceased production before the First World War, the last of the sailing vessels disappeared in 1939 and today there is no commercial traffic on the Bridgewater Canal. Once Runcorn was the country's leading centre for leather production. By 1968 all the tanneries had closed.

Since 1945 Runcorn has undergone another period of massive change. The renewal of the town centre saw the demolition of the streets and shops which were built in the early decades of the last century. This was followed by further large-scale clearances to make way for roads leading to the new Mersey road bridge. When Runcorn was designated a New Town in 1964, thirty-seven farms were taken for urban development and in order to create a single unified town, additional areas within old Runcorn were redeveloped. During the last thirty years the town and its environs have changed almost beyond recognition.

Many of the photographs are the work of professional photographers working in their studios. However, some of the pictures were taken by amateur photographers, two of whom merit special mention. Mr W.H. Mack, stationer of Runcorn, was interested in people and we are indebted to him for leaving us a valuable record of life in the town at the turn of the century. Mr Charles Timmins of the Bridgewater Foundry was another gifted amateur photographer who took many charming pictures of Runcornians at work and at play.

From a large collection of old photographs the author has attempted to present a balanced view of old Runcorn. Some pictures were chosen in order to illustrate important events, others simply to show period dress or traditional local customs. It is hoped that the book has recaptured something of the atmosphere of this unique Cheshire town in transition and that it brings back memories for old Runcornians as well as being a source of information for new Runcornians.

One
The Docks

Runcorn Docks in 1886. An everyday scene with dozens of schooners discharging cargoes of potters' materials for transhipment into narrowboats for Stoke-on-Trent via the Bridgewater and the Trent and Mersey canals. The schooners brought roofing slates from small ports in North Wales as well as pig iron from Scotland for the foundries of the Midlands. The little craft were maids of all work carrying roadstone, glassmaker's sand, chemical ores and scrap iron. Very few of the schooners displaced more than a hundred tons and yet with a crew of four or five seamen they frequently crossed the Atlantic to take Cheshire salt to the saltfish industry of Newfoundland. They would then carry the saltfish to Mediterranean ports where they would load fruit for Britain. Many small foreign sailing vessels arrived at Runcorn from Denmark, Holland, Belgium and Germany to load salt for their fishing industries. The other main export commodity of Runcorn docks was Lancashire coal.

The Runcorn registered schooner 'Gleaner' was typical of the small sailing vessels using the port. For many years she was engaged in carrying china clay and flints from ports in Devon and Cornwall. She was lost with her crew in the Irish Sea in November 1918.

The schooners 'Snowflake', 'M.E. Johnson', 'Englishman', and 'Dunvegan' at Runcorn in 1920. 'Snowflake' was probably the best known. She was built in Brundrit and Company's Mersey Street yard in 1880 and was still plying the Adriatic until a few years ago.

A river paddle-tug tows a schooner in the Ship Canal. The Bridgewater Trustees and their successors, the Bridgewater Company and the Manchester Ship Canal Company, provided free towage for sailing vessels to and from the estuary. Because of this Runcorn remained a sailing ship port into the 1930s.

Outward bound. Four sailing vessels are under tow on the upper Mersey. They will be released in fair winds at the estuary. The river tugs were essential to the success of the port of Runcorn and the first steamers built on the Mersey were constructed in local shipyards.

Runcorn Bridgewater Docks at the end of the last century. A three-masted barque lies alongside the Duke's warehouse with the china clay sheds seen in the background. Until the coming of the Manchester Ship Canal only the smaller sailing vessels could be towed through the tortuous Mersey sailing channels into Runcorn Docks. When the canal was opened for traffic much larger vessels could proceed to the docks via the canal regardless of the state of the tide in the upper river. Before the canal was built it was not unusual for a large vessel to have to wait eight or ten days in the estuary before a high tide enabled it to reach Runcorn. In 1894 in accordance with its enhanced status as an Urban District Council, the Runcorn Council adopted as its insignia, the symbol of a full-rigged ship, thus indicating that the town had become a deep water port within the new customs port of Manchester.

Mersey sailing flats under tow off Runcorn in 1906. Seen here are two of the larger two-masted 'jigger flats'. The flats were a familiar sight on the river from the eighteenth century. They were often equipped with conspicuous tan coloured sails.

Runcorn Docks before the Ship Canal was built. The 'Duker' paddle-tug 'Helen' assists a schooner alongside the pier at the Bridgewater Docks about 1885.

The 'Earl of Ellesmere' was the first of a class of powerful steamers built for the Bridgewater Trustees. She was launched in 1857 and was still in service nearly seventy years later. The 'Duker' tugs often towed twenty or more laden barges up river to Runcorn.

The Upper Mersey Navigation Commissioner's wooden buoy boat 'Preston' in about 1890. The little steamer was used to site over 120 navigation buoys in the upper Mersey's ever changing navigable channel. Piloting the river above Garston was never plain sailing and 'Preston' was employed in marking sandbanks shallows and wrecks which were hazards to craft making passage to Runcorn, Widnes and Weston Point Docks. Built at Brundrit and Whiteway's yard in 1867, the 42-ton 'Preston' operated on the river for 55 years. In addition to her buoy laying activities the vessel was employed as a supply tender to three light vessels which were on station between Garston and Ditton Brook.

Fishing smacks off Runcorn about 1905. In Victorian times there were over fifty inshore fishing boats registered at the port of Runcorn. They were employed in shrimping off the mouth of the River Dee and off the Lancashire coast. The boats displayed the letters RN signifying that they were registered at the Port of Runcorn.

Weston Point docks. Tall ships berthed at the Delamere dock of the river Weaver Navigation in about 1900.

Sailing vessels were a familiar sight at Runcorn even into the 1930s. Small coasting schooners arrived from ports great and small all round the coast of Britain. They came from Brixham Appledore, Lynmouth, Padstow, Bristol, Barrow and Glasgow. Others came from St. Petersburg, Riga, Rotterdam, Ostend and scores of ports in northern Europe.

Alongside at Runcorn Docks is the 100-ton three-masted schooner 'Harvest King' which was built in a local shipyard in 1879.

The large four-masted 2,400 ton steel barque 'Hougomont' is berthed at Runcorn lay-bye about 1908. Because the later sailing ships could not lower their steel top masts to pass under the railway bridge, they had to discharge their cargoes of grain into lighters at the lay-bye to the west of the bridge. The grain was then shipped to the millers at Warrington and Manchester. Before the First World War the tall ships brought whale oil for Runcorn's soapworks.

The coaster 'Moelfre Rose' was a constant visitor at Runcorn and Weston Point docks. She is seen discharging her cargo of china stone at Runcorn in the 1930s.

Schooners and steam vessels in Runcorn docks about 1905. During the nineteenth century few steamers were registered at the port of Runcorn. When the docks were crowded with small wooden sailing vessels with tarred rigging the presence of coal-burning craft could constitute a serious fire hazard.

Schooners at Runcorn docks about 1910. From left to right are the 'Irish Minstrel', 'Harvest King', unidentified and 'Sarah McDonald'. Many local people of quite modest means were prepared to invest their savings in sailing vessels and the ship's master was usually a principal shareholder in his schooner.

Because of the shallow and twisting nature of the sailing channels in the upper river, large sea-going craft could not proceed to Runcorn. As a result there developed in the nineteenth century, an immense barge traffic with trains of barges from Liverpool docks conveying considerable cargoes to Runcorn on every tide.

This photograph titled 'Dockland Shadows' was submitted for an exhibition of work by local amateur photographers held just before the last war. The schooner is the 'Mary Sinclair' which was the last locally owned sailing vessel to use the port of Runcorn. she was converted into a towing barge in 1936 and was broken up at the beginning of the war.

Two
The River Crossings

The view across to West Bank, Widnes during the construction of the Runcorn railway bridge. Work on the bridge began in 1863 and the project was completed in May 1868. The coming of the railway was a great benefit to Runcorn for, besides it linking the town to major cities, a vital branch line was constructed to the Bridgewater docks.

Building the arches of the railway bridge at West Bank, Widnes. The photograph was taken in May 1865.

The arches of the railway bridge under construction in 1866.

The completed bridge. The photograph was taken from the west side about 1870. The photographer positioned himself near to where Collier Street, Blantyre Street and Trentham Street are now situated. The farm was adjacent to what we now call No Mans's Land.

Mr Harrison, the last Runcorn ferryman, seen after his final crossing of the river. A fery service had been in operation since the twelfth century. It closed when the transporter bridge opened in 1905.

Runcorn ferry with the old public salt water bath house which was built in 1822. Belvedere Terrace and Clarence Terrace can be seen in the background. They were built to accommodate visitors who came to enjoy their summer holidays in pre-industrial Runcorn. The steam flour mill at Old Quay is at the left of the picture. The photograph was taken about 1885.

The construction of the transporter bridge. Sinking the cast iron cylinders for the bridge towers in June 1902.

The steel supporting towers of the transporter bridge nearing completion. They rose sixty-three metres above high water and were a landmark in the district for fifty-six years. The towers were bolted onto the cylinders which were fastened into solid rock twelve metres below the river bed.

The span of the transporter bridge under construction as viewed from the Widnes side of the river. The transporter bridge was built precisely where Telford had proposed to build his suspension bridge early in the nineteenth century. With a span of 333 metres the transporter was the same length as that put forward by Telford for his bridge.

Adjusting the cables at the anchorage of one of the transporter bridge towers in 1904.

Testing the transporter bridge. Five waggons loaded with casks of silicate and seven cart horses having a total weight of thirty-six tons are being used to test the bridge in May 1905.

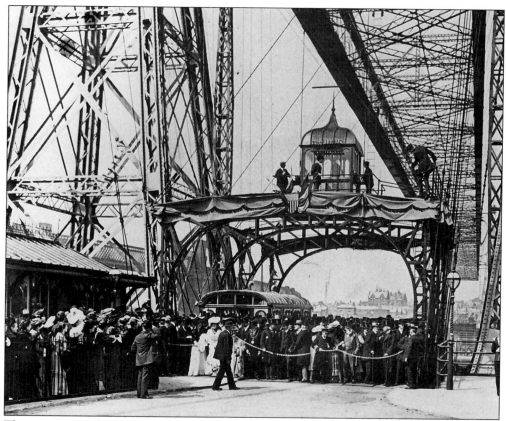

The transporter bridge was opened on May 29th 1905 by Sir John Brunner MP. The photograph shows the arrival of the car at Runcorn on the opening day. The car was capable of carrying four two-horse waggons and three hundred passengers. It took about two and a half minutes to cross the river and the Manchester Ship Canal. The car cleared the Ship Canal wall by about one and a half metres.

The transporter bridge took three and a half years to build at a cost of £137,000. It lost money during its first years of operation but by the 1940s traffic has increased to cause long queues to form on both sides of the river. The service did not operate after 11 p.m. and the bridge often closed during high winds. In the 1950s extensive repairs necessitated the closure of the bridge for some months. By 1950 the bridge was totally inadequate to cope with the increase in traffic and five years later work began on the present toll free road bridge.

Closing the gap. The new road bridge has made an enormous impact on the social and economic life of the district. It ended Runcorn's long period of isolation and its completion enabled the fields of north Cheshire to be developed for housing for people of Liverpool and Merseyside. The bridge was opened by Princess Alexandra of Kent on July 21st 1961.

A few months after this photograph was taken the new bridge was opened and work began on the demolition of the transporter bridge.

Three
The Ship Canal

Although the Manchester Ship Canal was dug with the aid of powerful steam excavators, thousands of navvies were employed in building the great seaway. By 1890 Runcorn's population had risen by nearly 6,000 as the navvies and their families found accommodation in the town. The arrival of the workforce meant good business for the local shopkeepers, licensees and lodging houses but the boom was short lived and very few of the navvies settled in the town when the canal was finished.

Many specialist Dutch workmen were employed during the building of the Ship Canal. Here crafstmen from Holland are engaged in fascine work to secure unstable ground on the canal embankment before the masonry could be placed in position. The photograph is believed to have been taken at Astmoor.

The Ship Canal wall, known locally as the gantry wall, is under construction in 1889. The old public salt water bath house is derelict as is Ditton Brook Ironworks which can be seen below the span of the railway bridge. Moored at the water's edge is the Runcorn ferryboat.

The drinks man. The large workforce employed on the Ship Canal works was in constant need of refreshment. Tea, coffee, beer and sandwiches were supplied to the men as they worked often in desolate marsh areas where food supplies were difficult to obtain. The drinks man is here plying his trade in Weston Point.

The gantry wall under construction. The work of building the canal seriously disrupted traffic to Old Quay docks. Local shipbuilding came to an end and for a number of years the Runcorn ferry service was suspended. The photograph was taken about 1890.

Noah's Ark Cafe provided food and beds for the navvies when they were working in areas where there were no shops or lodging houses. Here the cafe has been sited on Norton marsh.

Spectators view the progress of the Ship Canal construction from the pedestrian walkway on the railway bridge in 1892. The difficult curve of Runcorn Bend to the west of the bridge was widened in 1911 to allow the passage of larger vessels to Manchester.

Along the length of the Ship Canal 173 locomotives were employed with 6,000 waggons, each of seven tons capacity, on 230 miles of temporary railway track which twisted in and out, under and over and alongside everywhere. Two hundred horses were used to cart materials and in the removing of earth and rock. Here excavations are being carried out in the river bed beyond the dock entrance.

The flour mills at Old Quay await demolition in 1888.

The Old Quay Canal or Runcorn to Latchford Canal of the Mersey and Irwell Navigation Company is about to be swept away to make way for the Manchester Ship Canal. Old Quay flour mills and other canal side properties have been cleared to allow the excavation to begin.

Visitors come to see progress on the Canal. These privileged ladies pose for a souvenir photograph at Astmoor c.1890.

The Ship Canal works at Weston Point in 1891. In spite of the temporary closure of the docks at Runcorn and Weston Point trade was kept moving when the Ship Canal Company provided free towage facilities along the completed section of the waterway to Saltport. Barges were then used to carry cargo to Runcorn free of cost via the Runcorn and Weston Canal.

In the eighteenth century the Duke of Bridgewater constructed a narrow channel across Runcorn promintory in order that the ebb tides would be funnelled through the passage to scour away the silt which accumulated in front of the entrance to his canal. The 'Duke's Gut' is about to be demolished as excavators and spoil waggons are moved into position on No Man's Land c.1892.

Just as the work on the Ship Canal was nearing completion a large section of the sea wall in front of Runcorn Docks collapsed as water came into contact with a strata of rock in the foundations which contained salt. The damage was extensive and the loss of business considerable while repairs were being undertaken. The scale of the damage can be seen from the size of the two figures of workmen to the right of the centre of the picture.

A pleasure paddle steamer passes Wigg, Steel and Company's works a few months after the canal was opened. The canal was a boon to Wiggs as the factory acquired a wharf on deep water.

Loading salt the Salt Union's new wharf on the Ship Canal at Weston Point. This photograph of the heavily laden sailing flat 'Antigua' wsas taken about 1912.

The first of the tall ships came to Runcorn when the Ship Canal Company established a temporary port at the mouth of the River Weaver at Weston Point. Here large American timber ships are seen discharging cargo. When the Ship Canal was finished 'Saltport' was dismantled. The photograph was taken in 1892.

'Saltport' in 1892. Although the Ship Canal will not be opened to Manchester for another two years, this completed section of the waterway to Weston Point has become a busy port for large ocean-going ships.

A paddle-steamer proceeds to Manchester shortly after the opening of the canal in 1894.

Opposite: An impressive assembly. The mayors, aldermen, councillors and guests from towns which border the Ship Canal are seen at Runcorn on an excursion on the company's paddle-tug 'Dagmar' in the early 1920s.

Evidence of the severity of winter in the past. The coasting steamer 'Grampus' is held fast by the ice in the Ship Canal.

A large vessel loads salt at Salt Union's vacuum plant at Weston Point in 1913. The cargo is destined for Hakodate in Japan.

Barge traffic at Runcorn Docks at the turn of the century. Here the narrow beam Bridgewater Canal tug 'Warrington' assembles a train of barges to await the arrival of a larger 'Duker' river tug which will tow them to Liverpool.

Showing the flag. The transporter bridge car waits as H.M.S. 'Bristol' and her tugs make their way to Manchester. The 4,800-ton light cruiser was built in 1911 and during the First World War she served in the Mediterranean and the South Atlantic (photograph Michael Day Collection).

Assisted by tugs, the 'Charles Lykes' from Galvaston, Texas, is seen making her way to Manchester.

Weston Point at the turn of the century. Of the little group of dockside buildings seen here only Christ Church has survived to today. Prominent in the picture is Telford's sea wall which was built for the Trustees of the River Weaver Navigation Company about 1812.

Old Quay Dock and the locks of the Mersey and Irwell's Runcorn to Latchford Canal were removed to make way for the Ship Canal. The picture shows a tug, a sailing flat and a schooner at Old Quay yard in the 1920s.

The lock tender enjoys his pipe as he poses for his photograph at his shelter at the locks. A suggested date for the picture is 1895.

The old bucket dredger "Gowy" working in the Ship Canal in 1955. The canal and the river channel beyond the lock gates at Eastham required constant dredging at considerable expense to the company.

Four

The Bridgewater Canal

Narrowboat families pose shyly for a photograph on 'France' and 'Dee' in 1905. By the turn of the century over a thousand canal craft had been registered at the port of Runcorn. Many narrowboats were built in Runcorn's small shipyards and boat building yards.

Narrowboat folk on an ill-named boat a few years before the First World War. According to the census returns for 1851 some 454 boatmen and family members were living on canal craft at Runcorn and Weston Point on the day the census was taken. The boats carried unpleasant cargoes of bones, manure, night soil, chemicals and fertilizers. Only three or four persons were permitted to live in the little cabins and the boats were visited regularly by inspectors to see that the conditions of registration were being met.

A canal boatwoman leads her horse in Percival Lane about 1905. Although twenty-six narrow-beam tugs had been hauling craft on the Bridgewater Canal for many years, horse-drawn craft continued to be employed until well into this century.

Two narrowboats are passing up the lock staircase into the Bridgewater Canal. During the last century trade on the canal was considerable. In 1883 no less than 60,300 craft passed up and down the two lines of locks.

The 'Empress' cinema provides the backdrop to two narrowboats as they make their way towards Doctor's Bridge. The cosy cinema was demolished to make way for the approach road to the new Mersey road bridge.

Canal craft at the pottery crate warehouse at Bottom Locks c.1910. There were two lines of locks leading from the Bridgewater Canal down to the Ship Canal. One line was built by the Duke of Bridgewater in 1773. The 'new' line of locks was constructed in 1828. In the eighteenth century the lock staircase was considered one of the wonders of the age. Sightseers came from far and wide to watch the boats passing up and down the locks.

A scene near to Runcorn Town Bridge more often known as Savages Bridge or Doctor's Bridge. The two narrowboats are passing the town warehouse with the chimneys of Hazlehurst's soapworks visible in the background.

Washing day. A canal boatwoman draws water at a canal towing path stand-pipe in about 1900. Some boat families rented rooms in the town when their boats were tied up at Runcorn for a few days but generally canal folk did not mix with the local people. The picture was taken by Mr Mack about 1902.

A view looking down the old line of locks about ninety years ago. The Old Custom House of the port of Runcorn which was built when Runcorn first gained its independence from the port of Liverpool in 1847, can be seen to the right of the canal. The famous line of locks has been filled in and today it is difficult to appreciate the enormous importance of the system to Britain's commerce during the Industrial Revolution.

The end of an era. At Top Locks in the 1950s there were more pleasure craft than working boats. Here narrowboats are laid up awaiting disposal.

The Bridgewater Canal was still a busy waterway into the early 1930s. The narrowboats on the left of the picture were chiefly employed in carrying on the Trent and Mersey Canal which has locks of narrow gauge. The craft on the right of the photograph are larger river barges which were restricted to the Bridgewater Canal.

In the last days of commercial traffic on the Bridgewater Canal, Jonathan Horsefield's narrowboat 'Richard' is seen passing Cornes' Mill in May 1959.

Severe winters in Victorian times often saw the inland waterways frozen up for weeks and boatmen and their families suffered long periods of unemployment and hardship. The scene is Top Locks a hundred years ago.

Children from the narrowboats are seen against a background of potter's flints about 90 years ago. Because of the migratory nature of narrowboat life the children rarely spent more than a few days in any one school. They often carried their own school registers which recorded their spasmodic attendance at a dozen or more schools along the waterways of the country.

Narrowboats folk at Runcorn Docks in about 1905.

A silent scene at Top Locks in the late 1950s when the commercial traffic on the Bridgewater Canal had all but ceased. A couple of years later communication with the docks was severed when the lines of locks were filled in.

The Runcorn to Latchford or 'Old Quay Canal' of the Mersey and Irwell Navigation Company about 1880. This canal which was built in 1804, became a serious rival to the Bridgewater Canal. The Old Quay Canal was destroyed during the construction of the Manchester Ship Canal. The photograph looks east towards Wigg Works.

The Runcorn and Weston Canal was built in 1857 to link the Weaver Navigation to Runcorn Docks. The buildings are those of Salt Union's vacuum salt plant. The picture was taken about 1920.

Five
Churches and Chapels

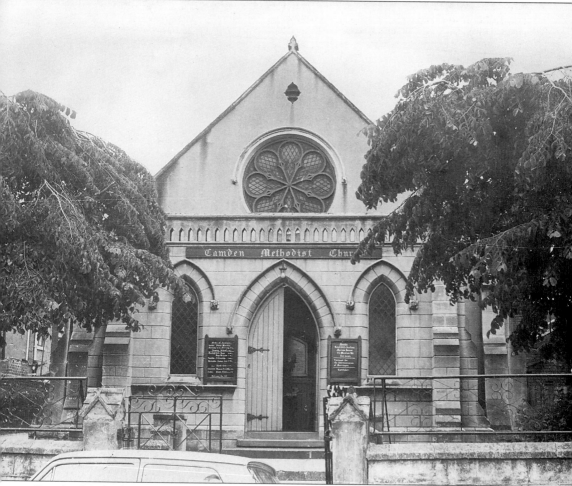

Camden Methodist church in Lowlands Road was the first of Runcorn's Wesleyan chapels built by Thomas Hazlehurst, the soap manufacturer in 1862. It was demolished for new bridge and road works in the 1960s. However, one of the rare weeping elms has survived the clearance.

Another of Mr Hazlehurst's gifts, Halton Road Methodist Church was built in 1871. It was closed about twenty years ago and was destroyed by fire whilst awaiting demolition.

Halton Road Methodist church. The splendid ceiling was a notable feature of the building.

St. Paul's Methodist church in High Street. Undoubtedly the finest building in the town centre, St. Paul's was built in 1866 at the huge cost of £8,000. Its grand Italianate colonnaded stone facade with its balconies and towers surmounted by domes dominated the town. Professor Ling who designed the New Town Master Plan, saw it as a building to be preserved as a link to the past. The church closed three years short of its centenary and after standing derelict for five years it was demolished in 1969. The town thus lost its one building of distinction.

St. Paul's in the days of large congregations and mighty choirs. The picture dates from 1907. The chapel offered perfect acoustics and during the Second World War famous singers and choirs performed concerts in aid of charity in the magnificent auditorium.

Weston Point Methodist chapel was built by Thomas Hazlehurst in 1872. The illustration is taken from a watercolour made shortly after its completion.

Methodism was established in Aston and Preston Brook after John Wesley preached there in 1781. The picture shows Aston Methodist chapel awaiting demolition to allow the site to be developed for a vast brewery which, in its turn, has since been demolished.

The old Brunswick chapel of 1827 was used as the British Restaurant during the last war. The building was pulled down in 1959.

The second St. Edward's R.C. church in Irwell Lane was opened in 1888 and was in use until the present St. Edward's opened in 1956. The old Irwell Lane church was demolished to make way for the New Town busway.

All Saints, the parish church of Runcorn, which was built in 1849 on the site of the medieval church, is evidence of the town's growing prosperity by the middle of the last century. All Saints was designed by Anthony Salvin, a famous Victorian architect who did much work on Windsor Castle. When describing the church the old guide books often refer to 'the immense accumulation of upright gravestones in the churchyard'.

St. Luke's Congregational chapel in Mason Street as it was before modernisation in the 1930s. St. Luke's was built in 1830. It was closed to make way for New Town development. The last service was held in April 1968.

Christ Church, Weston Point, was built by the Trustees of the River Weaver Navigation for their employees and their families in 1841. The Trustees were generous for they also built the minister's house, paid his stipend and made allowances to the church cleaners and the choristers. It is said that in Victorian times the church windows had to be covered because the lights were sometimes mistaken by ships' captains for that of the nearby lighthouse.

Repairs to the roof of St. Paul's Methodist church in 1906. During the work of renovation much decorative stonework was removed from the towers. Unfortunately, a fine plaster ceiling had to be sacrificied to enable the roof repairs to be carried out.

Archdeacon Alfred Maitland Wood was the vicar of All Saints, Runcorn from 1887 to 1911. He is seen at the door of the old Georgian manse which was on the site of the present vicarage in Highlands Road.

The Reverend Dr. William Preston was the vicar of Holy Trinity, Runcorn from 1872 to 1897. 'Daddy' Preston became renowned for his determination to bring to the altar unmarried couples and those migratory boat people who were living outside the sanctity of marriage. The photograph was taken from a Victorian magic lantern slide.

The ladies of St. John's Presbyterian Sunday School in 1895. Back row, left to right: Mrs Marion Faulkner, Mrs M. Prince, Mrs S. Hugues, Mrs T. Kirkham, Mrs Jessie Leach and Mrs E. Dutton. Third row: Mrs Bessie Moorfield, Mrs Florrie Littler, Mrs Richardson, Mrs Warburton, Mrs W. Leach and Mrs Booth. Second row: Mrs P. Hawkins, Miss Ada Booth, Miss S. Hayes, Mrs C. Baxter, unidentified, Miss Sophia Warburton, Mrs Thomas. Front row: Mrs Emily Pritchard, Miss Eva Baxter, Mrs J. Scragg, Mrs Louie Leach and Mrs Edith Barr.

This photograph of Camden Women's Meeting taken over a hundred years ago is perhaps the most striking picture of Victorian folk in the author's collection of photographs.

The Whit Monday walk by the town's Sunday Schools was the most popular event of the year. The ritual originated early in the last century and it grew until by the end of the century thousands were taking part. Dressed in their best clothes with church brass bands in attendance and accompanied by their teachers, clergy and the civic notables, the scholars paraded through the town with their banners. The photograph shows the Whit Walk of 1924.

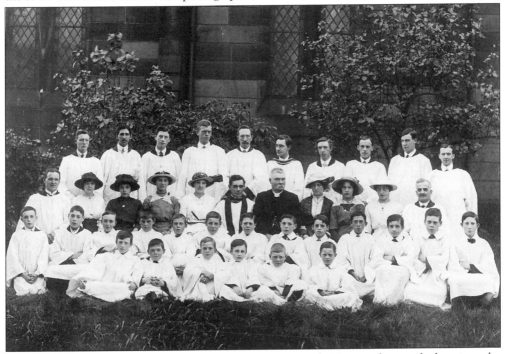

Every church once possessed a large choir. Seen here is Holy Trinity choir with the vicar, the Reverend C.R. Killick. The photograph was taken about 1920.

Camden Methodists in Regent Street en route to join the Whit Monday procession in the 1950s.

This picture of Holy Trinity choir dates from 1938. The vicar, the Reverend F. Coveney and the fully robed choir pose for a photograph before leaving to sing at Evensong in Chester Cathedral.

Six
The Industries

Women and girls dredge the mud for coal in the drained Bridgewater Canal at the Runcorn Soap and Alkali works. This factory at Savages Bridge was the first in Runcorn. It was built as a soapworks by John Johnson in 1803. Johnsons developed into a large firm and in 1865 it became the Runcorn Soap and Alkali Company producing basic chemicals. The works closed in the early 1930s.

The last schooner to be built at Runcorn was the 145-ton 'Despatch' seen here on the day of her launch in May 1886. 'Despatch' was one of the vessels employed in salt carrying to Newfoundland. She was in service for twenty-years before being wrecked off Holyhead in 1913.

The launch of a schooner was always a festive occasion and a carnival atmosphere prevailed on the day she left the slipway. Here 'Despatch' takes to the water. The construction of the Manchester Ship Canal ended shipbuilding at Runcorn and from 1889 no large coasting craft were built in the local shipyards.

Although shipbuilding ended with the coming of the Ship Canal, the repair of sailing vessels continued into the 1930s. The two-masted schooner 'Volant' is pictured undergoing a refit on Stubbs' slip in Old Quay yard in Mersey Road.

The schooner 'Redtail' on the stocks at Blundell and Mason's Belvedere Yard in 1867. 'Redtail' and her crew were lost in June 1917 probably as a result of war action.

Quarrying was a labour-intensive industry. In the middle of the last century when production was at its height, there were 750 men employed in John Tomkinson's Weston quarry. As the photograph shows, there was still a sizeable workforce in the quarry in the early years of this century.

To convey the stone to the stone loading wharfs and railway sidings at Weston Point, tramroads were constructed down the steep hillside. Although the quarries closed many years ago the line of the tramways can often be recognised in the pathways on Runcorn Hill. The picture shows a tramroad from Weston quarry in about 1908.

Opposite: The quarrying of Runcorn's red and pink sandstone was the first of the town's industries. There were quarries at Delph Bridge, the Stenhills, Mill Brow, Runcorn Hill and at Weston and Halton. Throughout the last century the stone was used over a wide area. Much of the fabric of Chester Cathedral and that of the medieval church of St. Mary at Nantwich was restored using Runcorn or Weston stone and many of the churches and public buildings in our district are of the local stone. The illustration shows a local quarry in the last years of the nineteenth century.

An old motor lorry has been adapted to serve as a locomotive in a Weston quarry in the 1920s (photograph, Industrial Railway Society. H.W. Robinson collection).

Another view of the Weston quarry tramroad. Occasionally the empty trucks were used to carry coal and machine parts up to the pumping engine at the waterworks on Runcorn Heath. The Weston quarry was the last to close in 1942. Over the years all the old quarries were filled with industrial waste and domestic refuse and the sites have been landscaped to become the attractive recreational areas of Rock Park and Runcorn Hill.

Some very large blocks of stone were cut in the Runcorn and Weston quarries. The great columns of the porticos of some of Cheshire's stately homes were fashioned from single blocks of the local stone. The massive masonry of Perch Rock Battery, the estuary fort at New Brighton, was quarried at Runcorn as was much of the stone used in the building of Liverpool docks.

Quarrying was heavy, dangerous work often resulting in serious accidents. Here quarrymen manhandle a large block of stone onto a truck in Weston quarry in the early years of this century.

Messrs Timmins and Sons, engineers and iron founders of the Bridgewater Foundry at Delph Bridge, was established in 1827. The firm enjoyed a considerable reputation not only for the excellence of its engineering products but also for its expertise in artesian well boring. At one time there were over 200 employees engaged in the manufacture of air compressors, pumping engines, winding engines and diving apparatus as well as machinery required in the soap and chemical works. Timmins foundry and engineering works closed about ten years after the Second World War.

Thirsty work. Moulders at work in Timmins foundry. The men needed a constant supply of beer which was supplied to them from the nearby 'Bull's Head' and the 'Moulder's Arms'.

Workmen employed in shovelling moulding sand at Timmins foundry in about 1910.

The packing department of Hazlehurdt's soapworks in High Street in the early years of the century. The works was established by Thomas Hazlehurst in 1816 and within fifty years the firm had acquired a world reputation. In late Victorian times Hazlehurst's 'Anchor' blue mottled soap, 'Bouquet', 'Pearl', 'Skylark', 'Antelope', 'Balloon' and other soaps were winning medals for excellence at international exhibitions in Paris, Calcutta, Australia and New Zealand. The firm also produced wax candles, nightlights and Eau de Cologne. When Hazlehursts became part of Lever Brothers, soap making at the Runcorn works ended just before the First World War.

The soap makers' vats at Hazlehursts. By the middle of the last century the manufacture of soap was Runcorn's premier industry and before the duty on soap was removed in 1853 the town's soaperies were contributing £80,000 a year to the national exchequer.

Hazlehursts realised the importance of attractive presentation and their products were packaged in colourful wrappings. The illustration is taken from one of the firm's advertising displays.

Salt Union vacuum plant. In 1882 a pipeline was laid to carry brine from Marbury near Northwich to a refinery built at Weston Point. Within a few years the enterprise had expanded to become a major industry in Runcorn. In 1911 a new plant was installed for the vacuum evaporation of brine which vastly increased production. The photograph shows conveyer belt loading taking place at Salt Union about 1920.

Bagging salt at the vacuum plant at Salt Union. In 1937 Salt Union became part of I.C.I.

The tubes are being cleared of scale during a brief shut down at Salt Union's vacuum plant. Because of the intense heat the men could work only for a few minutes at a time.

Astmoor Tannery in 1961. Tanning was a small-scale industry in the Runcorn area in the eighteenth century. However, by 1865 it had become big business and the industry was to grow to become the major source of employment in Runcorn. According to local folklore, an early tannery at Astmoor supplied leather to make the boots used by the Duke of Wellington's army during the Napoleonic war.

Highfield Tannery was the largest of the tanneries and like all Runcorn's early industries it was sited on the canal. It was via the waterway that Highfield received its coal supplies and also the hides and tanning materials from the port of Liverpool. Highfield was the last of the town's tanneries to close in 1968.

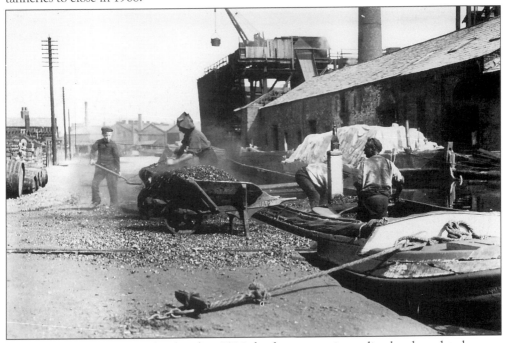

When Hazlehurst's soapworks closed in 1914 the factory was immediately adapted to become Camden Tannery. The tannery obtained its coal from narrowboats and the picture is looking east along the Bridgewater Canal towards Delph Bridge. Camden was the first tannery to close in 1958.

Work on the tan pits was heavy and unpleasant. Here men labour on the pits at Highfield Tannery. Eighty years ago Runcorn was the country's leading centre for the production of leather. Five large tanneries made a vital contribution to the war effort in two World Wars and they saved the town from the worst effects of recession and unemployment between the wars.

A shoulder roller is in operation at Highfield Tannery in the 1960s. The use of man-made substitutes for leather brought about a rapid decline in the industry from about 1955.

Puritan Tannery was the most modern of the tanneries. Its Halton Road premises were designed by the architect who planned Wembley Stadium. The illustration shows the tannery's bend half sole sorting room.

For longer wear and greater comfort . . .

PURITAN
Leather Soles

PURITAN TANNERIES LTD · RUNCORN · CHESHIRE

At one time this famous Puritan advertisement could be seen all over Britain. It was displayed on most of the country's railway stations.

The Evans Biological Institute. Evans, Sons, Lescher and Webb Biological Institute was established at Crofton Lodge in 1911. The company produced antitoxins, sera, vaccines and chemotherapeutic substances. The firm's products were used to combat diphtheria, tetanus, typhoid, cholera and plague and it was one of the leading world concerns in the field of sera and vaccines. The picture shows the Institute about 1936.

The stables at the Evans Biological institute. The horses which were used in the production of anti-toxins were provided with the best conditions and were turned out to pasture in the surrounding meadows.

Opposite: The Analytical Laboratory at the Evans Biological Institute. The Institute was closed in the 1970s and housing estates now occupy the site of the laboratories, stables and the adjoining farm. Seen in this photograph of 1937 are, left to right: Jimmy Collins, Olga Sinclair, George Shaw, Ernie Jolley, Fred Rymill and Jack Whitney.

Not all the horses at Evans Medical Supplies were kept for the production of sera and anti-toxins. 'Titch', shown here, was the firm's working horse which sometimes represented the company in the Runcorn Carnival.

The workforce of the Australian Alum Company in 1910. The works, which was sited next to Highfield Tannery, manufactured alum and sulphate of alum which were used in the preparation of medicines and cosmetics and also in paper making, paint manufacture and in water purifying processes. Note the works' cat on the front row.

An evil smelling cargo. A shipment of animal hornes from the meat canning factories in Brazil is piled on the quay at Runcorn docks. The horns are required for the manufacture of fertilizer. In the foreground is a cargo of pig iron probably destined for the foundries of the Midlands. The photograph was taken about 1885.

The quay areas of the docks at Runcorn were always covered with great piles of potters' material awaiting transhipment by narrowboat to Stoke-on-Trent. Here lump china stone is being discharged.

'Gladys' was one of a number of industrial locomotives employed in Castner-Kellner's works at Weston Point. The picture was taken in 1917.

Castner-Kellner works when it was still surrounded by farmland in 1906. The factory which began operations in 1897 has been a mainstay of employment in the town. Castners was responsible for the rapid development of Weston Point when a large estate of company houses was built between 1921 and 1932.

The Manchester Ship Canal's Sprinch boatbuilding and repair yard at the Big Pool on the Bridgewater Canal was claimed to be the finest of its type in Britain. The yard was responsible for the maintenance of over two hundred canal craft. The employees pose for a photograph c.1924. Top row: Frank Lovell, John Moores, Tom Mather. Row 4; Tom Mears, Edgar Wilkinson, FRanck Burton, Norman Holt, Bob Boardman, Franck Hurst. Row 3: Frank Rushton, Arthur Lightfoot, George Jackson, Edward Ramsden, Bill Hoxworth, Jack Povey, Frank Faulkner, Wally Woodward, Joe Dale. Row 2: John Shallcross, Len Tomlinson, Bill Littler, Bob Sewel, ? Jones, Arthur Marsh, Henry Rone, Jack Rowlinson, Dick Pidcock (Snr.), Sam Royle. Front row: Herman Terreta, Bill Eastup, John Ashcroft, Jack Hampson, Tom Rodgerson, Dick Pidcock, Alf Ramsden, Ernie Green, Frank Urmson.

The Castner-Kellner factory in Weston Point has outlasted all the other chemical works established in Runcorn. In 1926 the factory became part of I.C.I. The photograph dates from about 1918.

This old wall is a reminder of Runcorn's industrial past for the coping stones were once the sleeper blocks of an early nineteenth century tramway. The rails were laid from Mill Brow quarry, across Sutton Street, Malcolm Street and Heath Road to a stone-loading wharf on the Big Pool. In the picture the Pool has been drained to allow the construction of the access road to the new Mersey road bridge.

Seven
Sport and Leisure

Runcorn Mandolin Band about 1903. Two of the adults have been identified. Miss Temperley, the organiser and leader is the the violinist at the centre of the picture and Miss Bertha Heath is standing at the right of the photograph. One or two local families still possess the musical instruments seen in the picture.

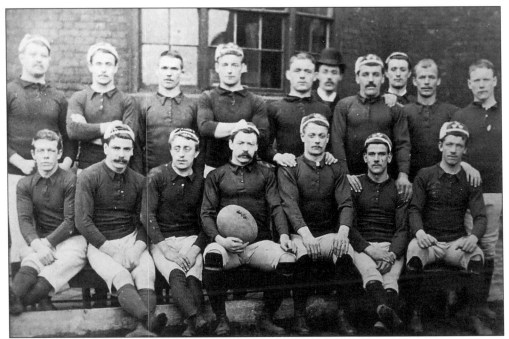

Runcorn Rugby Union Club in 1888. Rugby Union Football was played at the Canal Street ground until 1895 when the club left the Rugby Football Union to join the professional Rugby League. During the First World War Rugby League football ceased to be played at Runcorn. Since then soccer has replaced rugby although there was a brief revival of Rugby League in the 1980s when Runcorn Highfield R.L. Club shared the ground with the town's soccer club.

The Runcorn Parish Church Handbell Ringers in the early years of this century. They are J. Cropper and F. Walsh (seated) and T. Mather, W. Stubbs, B. Trevitt and L. Roberts.

A Brunswick Methodist concert party in formal pose. Because of the costumes it is difficult to venture a date for the picture but it is thought that the occasion was a rehearsal for a concert to celebrate the coronation of King Edward VII and Queen Alexandra in 1901.

The cycling club outing. In late Victorian times Runcorn boasted two cycling clubs, the 'Sons of Temperance Cycling Club' and the 'Cycling Touring Club'. The latter used the 'Wilsons Hotel' in Bridge Street as its headquarters.

Planning the route. Members of a Runcorn cycling club rest at Daresbury during a trip into the countryside. This charming picture was taken by Mr Charles Timmins.

Runcorn cyclists rest at Walton about ninety years ago.

The Halton Ladies' Annual Walk. The Halton Women's Friendly Society was started in 1815. Every year the Ladies' Club held a procession through Halton Village. This became the main social event in the village for over a hundred years. After a service at St. Mary's church, the ladies, dressed in their best attire, wearing blue sashes and carrying white staffs, walked in procession to the Parish boundary in Halton Road. The walk was always led by Lady Brooke and the occasion ended with a tea party and children's sports at Halton Castle.

The men of Halton are spectators at the annual Ladies' walk in 1905. In the evening there would be fireworks and dancing within the walls of the castle. The final procession took place in 1920.

Members of the Preston Book Brass Band pose for a formal photograph after accompanying the Halton Ladies' Walk of 1893.

After the Ladies' Walk. There was a serious reason for the establishment of the Ladies' Club for the society provided funds from which the members could claim benefit for death grants, maternity allowance and assistance during times of hardship.

The ladies of Halton in procession in 1893. They were always accompanied by various brass bands. On this occasion the Preston Book band has the honour of providing the music. The village Main Street is little changed at this spot in the hundred years that have passed since the walk of 1893.

An Edwardian tea party. Relatives of Sir Richard Brooke assemble at Norton Priory on the occasion of his twenty-first birthday.

Mrs Mercer's private school in Irwell Lane in 1907. The establishment was intended mainly for delicate children. The author met two of the children seen here when they were in their eighties!

The Charles Tonks Quadrille Band in the 1920s. Seen here are John Worsley (bass), Jack Povey (flute), Ralph Dykes (violin), Charles Tonks (band leader and pianist), John Clare (cornet), George Hill (cello), ? Jones (violin) and ? Wheeler (drums). The band was together from 1915 to about 1930. Mr Tonks was a painter and decorator with a shop in Church Street.

The band of the Runcorn Volunteers (The Second Battalion of the Cheshire Rifle Volunteers) display their trophy which they won at the Cottage Hospital Festival in 1891.

The ladies-in-waiting and their attendants in Mr Rigby's photographic studio before taking part in the parade in a Runcorn Festival about 1930.

The Runcorn Festival of 1930. The ladies-in-waiting and the train bearers pose for their photograph after their dress rehearsal in Holy Trinity School in Pool Lane.

Camden Sunday School's Ali Baba and the Forty Thieves parade in Lowlands Road in a Carnival in the early 1950s.

The Oddfellows tableau. By 1830 Runcorn had branches of a number of Friendly Societies. These included the Ancient Order of Foresters, the Ancient Order of Shepherds and the Rechabites. The picture shows the tableau presented by the Rose of Sharon Lodge of the Grand Order of Oddfellows at a carnival in the 1930s.

The Runcorn and Widnes Co-operative Society Gala of 1926. The float advertising bakery products wins first prize. The old King's cinema can be seen in the background.

The Runcorn Festival Queen with her attendants in 1930. Brenda, the Queen, is attended by Mrs Breadnam, Cicely Breadnam and Joyce Clews.

Camden Sunday School present 'Britain Down the Ages' at the Runcorn Carnival in 1948. The procession is seeen arriving at the Canal Street football ground.

The annual Runcorn Festival or Carnival was held to raise funds for the Cottage Hospital. It was held under the auspices of the Runcorn Council with the first one taking place in 1926. The Festival was always a spectacular event with hundreds taking part in the great procession. The Sunday Schools, day schools, the organised youth movements and the workpeople from the local firms paraded through the town to the Canal Street football ground where there were sideshows and dancing, The Carnival attracted thousands of spectators. Mr Matthew Thomas who had a grocer's shop in Balfour Street often led the procession in his capacity as 'mounted marshal'.

The Halton Rose Fete. This annual event culminated in a parade of floats, brass bands and fancy dress revellers in the lanes of the village. Increased traffic generated by the New Town brought about the end of the Rose Fete. The picture of the Rose Queen and her retinue was taken in 1927.

The Runcorn Festival of 1928. The Queen, Ida Wardle and the previous year's queen, Edna Rushton, with their attendants in what are now the town hall grounds.

The Runcorn Pioneer Band in the 1960s. In the late Victorian times there were at least a dozen drum and pipe and brass bands in the town. The Runcorn Harmonic Band and the bands of the churches, the Friendly Societies and the Rifle Volunteers all provided music on festive occasions. Before the last war the Runcorn Pioneer Band and those of the organised youth movements together with the local jazz bands accompanied the floats in the Carnival procession.

The Runcorn County Secondary School ('The Tech') scouts with their scoutmaster, Mr H.S. Stalker, about 1922.

The staff of the 'Palace', which became the 'Scala', in the late 1920s.

The Chairman of the Council, Councillor Thomas Clare is amused by Alderman Gittins' observations at a tree planting ceremony to celebrate the coronation of George VI and Queen Elizabeth in May 1937.

Astmoor AFC display their trophies. Shortly after this happy occasion the team suffered a great tragedy when the star player, Roy Williamson (middle row, fourth from the left) died of anthrax which he contracted at his work in the tannery in 1928. Although most of the houses in Astmoor were only built between the wars, the little community was swept away by New Town development in the 1970s.

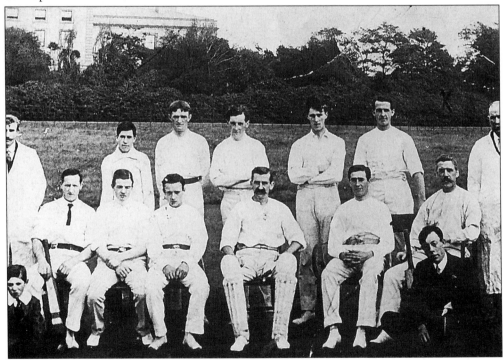

Norton Priory staff cricket team seen with the house in the background about 1910.

Eight
Some Old Runcornians

During the late Victorian decades and in the early years of this century, Dr John Robinson was the best known of Runcorn's physicians. A kindly man who 'forgot' to send bills to poor patients, Dr Robinson was renowed for his ferocious medicines. In his youth he was an exercise fanatic who walked prodigious distances. To children he affected a stern, gruff manner which did not conceal his generous disposition and they delighted in hiding his bowler hat when he came to visit them. The good doctor always carried a small pair of pliers in his pocket for instant on-the-spot dentistry. A shabby but much respected bachelor, Dr Robinson was the son of Pastor William Robinson who was the first minister at St. Luke's Congregational Chapel in Mason Street in the 1830s.

Captain William Durepaire of the Runcorn schooner 'Redtail' with a member of his crew in 1917. The vessel and her crew were lost later in the year.

One of Mr Mack's photographs of local people. This study was titled 'The Pig feeder'. It was probably taken about 1900.

Another of W.H. Mack's pictures. The photograph of the carter has been carefully arranged but he is anonymous and we have no idea of the place or date of the picture. The photograph was submitted for an exhibition of work by local amateur photographers.

Throughout the war years up until the advent of television Runcorn was noted for its enthusiastic amateur dramatic societies. Halton Road Methodists, Holy Trinity players, Camden Methodists, St. John's Presbyterian A.D.S., Greenway Road Methodists and the I.C.I. Recreation Club A.D.S. all presented plays to appreciative audiences. Here, St. John's pause for a photograph during the dress rehearsal of Moliere's play 'The Miser'. The players are, front row: Peter Johnson, Irene Shuttleworth, Beryl Walker, Sheila Kelly, Bill Dutton. Second row: Malcolm Williamson, Laurence Griffiths, Bert Starkey, Theodore Trezise, John Howie, Fred Hopkins and Ron Stephens.

Volunteers for the Boer War. This photograph, taken in 1899, shows six Runcorn volunteers ready to leave for South Africa. Colour-sergeant John Whitehead, an old scholar of the Parish School, was killed in action the day before the relief of Ladysmith.

Local soldiers returning from leave are seen off by their families at Runcorn railway station during the first World War.

Off for a day at the seaside. Local trippers are seen enjoying an outing by charabanc in 1925.

During the construction of the Ship Canal Runcorn's population increased as thousands of navvies and their families settled in the district. There was pressure on the schools and to provide extra places a little Roman Catholic School was built in Weston village in 1889. When the canal was finished the workforce moved on and the roll of the school fell until it was no longer viable. It closed in 1902 and the building was bought by Sir John Brunner who presented it to the people of Weston as their village hall. The building is today the headquarters of the Weston scouts.

In the first World War the Parish Church Vicarage in Highlands Road was used as an emergency hospital and some 3,460 wounded servicemen were treated there. Here soldiers and nurses are seen with Canon Perrin in his chaplain's uniform in the vicarage grounds in 1917.

Local police officers and special constables seen at a social occasion in the Second World War.

Highfield and Camden Tanneries' Ex-servicemens' reunion dinner held at the Baths Hall on 8th November 1946.

Marbles in Halton Main Street at the turn of the century. The rural character of the village is enphasised by the cows being taken through the street. Although the little lodge gatehouse to Norton Priory remains, the fields on both sides of Main Street have been built over and what was once an isolated village community is now at the heart of Runcorn New Town.

Nine
Town and Country Views

Halton Grange was built by the soap manufacturer, Thomas Johnson, in 1856. The mansion was bought by his rival, Thomas Hazlehurst in 1874. In 1909 the house became the home of Francis Boston of the Puritan Tannery. It was acquired by the Runcorn Council for £2,250 together with some 12 acres of land in 1932 to become Runcorn's new town hall. The transaction was denounced by the local press as 'squandermania' during a period of severe economic depression.

Ancient houses in Pool Lane. In the eighteenth century Pool Lane was known as Sour Milk Lane or Buttermilk Lane and it was at the centre of the village.

Another view of old properties in Pool Lane.

The Castle Hotel at Halton was formerly the courthouse of the Duchy of Lancaster. It was built from the stones of the castle gatehouse in 1738.

Runcorn's first town hall and bridewell was built in 1831 at a cost of £450. A few years ago the industrial grime of more than a century was removed from this building of some architectural merit.

The New Inn in High Street seen when it still retained its original facade dating from the early years of the last century. In the Regency period the town's Friendly Societies held their meetings here. The appearance of the old inn has been much altered over the years and it has been renamed to become the Old Bridge Inn.

The imposing Mill House at the junction of Heath Road and Halton Road was once the home of the Timmins family. During the last war it was used by the army for billeting purposes. The house was pulled down shortly after the war and the site became the Festival Gardens. Later the land was developed for housing.

The original Weaver Hotel in Weston Point. At one time the hotel was a packet house which was used by the Trustees of the River Weaver Navigation Company so that they could recover small coin with which to pay their employees.

Halton Lodge was built by the industrialist Charles Wigg. Known to modern Runcornians as Grice's Farm, the house was demolished some years ago and a school was built on the site. The old gateposts to Halton Lodge are all that remain of this large house. It is seen here decked in bunting for the coronation of the present queen.

Ship Cottages which were next to the Ship Inn in Mill Brow, were typical examples of Runcorn's early nineteenth century housing. The cottages were constructed of stone quarried in nearby Mill Brow quarry - now Rock Park.

The Bull's Head in Halton Road a few days after it closed its doors for the last time.

The Old Hall in Weston Village was built in 1607. The medieval preaching cross was restored to celebrate the Diamond Jubilee of Queen Victoria in 1897.

Back High Street about seventy years ago. The householder is seated outside what is now the Curiosity Bookshop. In the background are the houses of Princess Street.

Once the homes of Bridgewater Canal employees, these canalside cottages near to Delph Bridge are awaiting demolition in the 1970s.

The first St. Edward's Roman Catholic church in Runcorn was built in Windmill Street in 1846. From 1888 the building was used as classrooms for St. Edward's school. The building was demolished in 1981.

The heart of old Runcorn looking up Bridge Street towards the market hall. At the edge of the left of the photograph is the town hall and police station. Behind the fountain Handley and Beck's shop still retains its Georgian features. A hundred years ago the short stretch of Bridge Street to the left of the fountain was often known as Runcorn Street.

Another view of the centre of old Runcorn taken about 1905.

Gilbert Street, off Percival Lane, was one of the first streets to be built near to Runcorn Docks. The houses were built in the late eighteenth century for the employees of the Duke of Bridgewater.

Percival Lane. Once a busy thoroughfare to Runcorn Docks, Percival Lane has been isolated by modern development and the houses seen here are long gone. It was said that at one time there were so many pubs in Percival Lane that if a thirsty seaman took a thimble of beer at the one nearest to the docks then doubled the quantity at every pub as he went up the lane, he would be incapably drunk before he reached Top Locks.

High Street. The imposing twin towers of St. Paul's church dominate High Street. Lea's ironmomger's shop is at the right of the picture at the corner of Church Street.

High Street looking east. The site once occupied by St. Paul's church is now St. Paul's Health Clinic.

Runcorn Market was built in 1856. It became the public swimming baths early this century. The illustration shows the market hall before alteration.

The Parish School is the oldest in Runcorn. It was established as the National School in 1811. When the old building was pulled down the stone inscription from "Proverbs" which was above the entrance was salvaged to be built into the wall of the new All Saints Primary School.

Bridge Street about ninety years ago.

A pavement pot seller displays his wares in Bridge Street about 1904.

Extensive advertisement hoardings were a feature of Victorian towns. Here a bill poster is seen at work on Savages Bridge in 1891.

Rock Mount, Heath Road at the turn of the century. Most of the folk who were living in these cottages made a living by making boiled sweets to be sold in the markets or they potted shrimps to be sold in the public houses of the town. A garage and car showroom now occupy the site.

Greenway Road in 1900. This quiet Lane was to become a busy main road to Chester and the south after the transporter bridge was opened in 1905.

Water Street in the 1930s. Exactly a hundred years before this photograph was taken cholera raged in the tiny cottages in the narrow streets of the district. In Victorian times the area was known as the 'Rookery' - a crowded and unhealthy neighbourhood where typhoid, smallpox and diphteria were endemic.

These old houses in King Street were built on Cooper's Meadow and they date from Runcorn's expansion as an industrial town in the early years of the last century.

When Victorian Runcorn expanded across the Bridgewater Canal, an area of housing known as Newtown came into being. Shaw Street C. of E. school was built to serve the district. The school was demolished when the road system to the new Mersey Bridge was being built in the 1960s.

Brunswick Street. All traces of Brunswick Street disappeared with the renewal of the shopping area of Church Street and the clearance of old streets in the Mersey ward.

Lea's corner, Church Street. Lea and Sons was a long established local engineering firm. The company specialised in the manufacture of hydraulic engines and high pressure apparatus as well as producing oxygen and hydrogen. In 1925 when drilling within the works, the company discovered 'A radium spring which possesses curative properties particularly effective in cases of gout, rheumatism, asthma, anaemia and even weak eyesight. Bottles are sent to all parts of the kingdom'. The radio-active water could be bought at the company's ironmonger's shop seen here. Lea's corner was demolished when Church Street was renewed after the war.

Mr Matthew Thomas at the door of his grocer's shop in Balfour Street. Mr Thomas is the mounted Viking seen in the carnival on page 102.

High Street in the days before motor traffic. The buildings have changed little over the years since the photograph was taken.

Bridge Street at the turn of the century. Narrowboat women are shopping at a grocer's stall. Hygienic conditions are not the best with bacon, sausage and cheese on open display.

CHURCH ST. RUNCORN.

In the early 1920s the Manchester Ship Canal Company presented to the town a strip of land which bordered the canal and the new Mersey Road construction was undertaken in 1924. The project provided work for many unemployed local men.

Opposite: Church Street looking towards High Street. Brunswick Street is to the left. The photograph was taken about 1908.

Runcorn's old Custom House which was built in 1847 and the adjoining properties were pulled down when the lock pools were filled a few years ago.

The fountain in Bridge Street was a feature of the old town centre for more than a hundred years. It was given by the Earl of Ellesemere in the 1850s. The fountain was removed to allow for road widening.

Runcorn Technical Institute in Waterloo Road was built in 1894 with Sir John Brunner being a generous provider of financial help. The building later became the Runcorn County Secondary School ('The Tech') which provided grammar school education until the move to Helsby after the last war.

Highlands Road c.1910. Higher Runcorn was a detached community separate from the rest of the town until the early years of the century when Runcorn expanded to the south.

Pool Lane awaits the bulldozers. The car is parked outside the 'George' public house which served the last drink in 1928.

A hundred years ago Heath Road was a quiet country lane off which Thomas Johnson built his grand mansion in the style of Queen Victoria's Osborne House in the Isle of Wight. Halton Grange remains but the Big Pool has gone and the fields have become a residential area.

This hundred year old photograph shows the remnants of Rocksavage, the great Elizabethan house of the Savage family, which was built in 1568. In 1617 King James I and his retinue stayed at Rocksavage after a day's hunting in Halton deer park.

This magazine illustration from an article written early in the century claims that the thatched Abbey Cottage off Mersey Road was 'the oldest cottage in England'.

The alms-houses on Halton Hill were founded by Pusey Brooke in the eighteenth century for the retired servants of the Brooke family. They were nearly two hundred years old when they were demolished in the 1960s.

Christ Church Vicarage in Weston Point was built by the Trustees of the River Weaver Navigation Company. The picture was taken about sixty years ago.

Church Street in Edwardian days. Little has changed since the picture was taken but Dennis Brundrit's neo-gothic house lost its mock medieval features when it was modernised to become the South Bank Hotel some years ago.

Norton Priory was the home of the Brooke family from 1545. The first house was built from the stones of the abbey. The house shown here replaced the Tudor building about 1730. The Brookes left the district in 1921 and seven years later the Norton Priory mansion was demolished.

This splendid facade to Hallwood, Sir John Chesshyre's house at Halton, was pulled down after becoming unsafe as a result of bombing during the war. Sir John was the Premier Sergeant-at-Law to King George II. Hallwood is now the Tricorn public house.

The overgrown gardens and the ruined Dutton Workhouse photographed in 1973. The workhouse was designed to accommodate 232 poor folk. It was built in 1857 at a cost of £7,500.

Greenway Road Primitive Methodist Chapel and its schoolroom were built in 1871. The site was required for the approach road to the new Mersey road bridge. The picture was taken a few months before its demolition in the 1960s.

For many years between the wars this old tank was a feature on Runcorn Park.

A view looking down Bridge Street towards the town hall with Ellesemere Street to the left. Opposite is the open market.

Until its demolition in the 1960s the Hill School on Halton Hill was the Sunday School and parish hall for St. Mary's church. When the elevated site was acquired by the North West Water Authority as the possible location for a reservoir, the resulting compensation settlement enabled St. Mary's to build a fine new parish hall.

A stone-built thatched cottage on The Green in Halton village. The large sign painted on the castle walls is an advertisement for the Castle Hotel and Recreational Grounds. The castle ruins were reduced by the collapse of a large section of masonry in 1913 about ten years after this photograph was taken.

The Old Hall in High Street was built in the seventeenth century. It was demolished to make way for the Salvation Army's Citadel in 1883. On the site today is the Trustee Savings Bank.

This well-known study of Crescent Row was taken by Mr Mack just after the turn of the century.

A unique institution. This old postcard depicts the Runcorn Grappling Corps operating near Savages Bridge. When the town's waterways were busy, death from drowning was a remarkably frequent occurrence. In the first four years of its existence this voluntary organisation recovered fifty-two bodies from the docks and canals in the town.

Holloway was once a cartway which connected the town to the outlying district of Higher Runcorn. The photograph shows that it was still a country lane in 1900.

The girls in the Runcorn Steam Laundry pose for their photograph about ninety years ago. The laundry was situated above Savages Bridge.

A royal visit in 1925. King George V crosses the transporter bridge on a brief visit to Runcorn on his way to Chester races. He is being greeted by Alderman Gittins, the Chairman of the Runcorn Urban District Council.

Runcorn War Memorial. The ceremony of unveiling the monument on November 14th 1920. The cross was unveiled by Colonel Bromley Davenport, the Lord Lieutenant of Cheshire, at the invitation of the Chairman of the Council, Mr R.H. Posnett. The prayers of dedication were read by the vicar, the Revd. H.N. Perrin, the first wreath was laid by Major G.F. Ashton. M.C. whilst Mrs Posnett placed a wreath on behalf of the people of Runcorn. An enormous crowd estimated at 10,000 people attended the ceremony to remember the four hundred local men who died in the war. Twenty-eight years later on November 7th 1948, additional panels were unveiled to reveal the names of 120 service personnel who died in the Second World War.

Court dwellings. During the last century Runcorn possessed many unhealthy courts such as Lowe's Court off Cooper Street seen here. The courts were often named after slum landlords and the tiny dwellings lacked even the basic necessities such as sanitation and a water supply.

Pool Hollow off Heath Road. This rural setting was to remain quiet countryside until the spread of housing in the years immediately before the last war.

The 'Theatre Royal' is destroyed by fire in 1906. The wooden theatre could hold about 1,200 patrons. Although it was called 'The Blood Tub' because of the frequency of its tragic melodramas, Shakespearian productions were often staged. The theatre was situated in Duke Street. It was built in 1868 and as can be seen on the bill-board in the photograph, the last presentation was 'Silent Witness'.

The Lock Pool. Two reservoirs or lock pools were sited adjacent to the old line of locks on the Bridgwater Canal. They were an attractive feature of Dukesfield until they were filled in the 1960s.

A funeral in 1911. Led by the police superintendent and the leading dignitaries of the town, the impressive funeral procession of Mr W. Timmins, a notable local industrialist proceeds up Greenway Road. Briscoe and Sadler's grocer's shop later became that of the Monks family who are still prominent grocers in Runcorn.

Opposite: Waterloo Road in the 1920s. Although this was the main road leading to the transporter bridge and the only road to Widnes and the north, there was little evidence of traffic when the photograph was taken.

This biplane caused much excitement when it landed in a field at Grice's farm at Halton Lodge. It was said that the pilot came to visit the farmer's daughter.

Stone Street, off Bridge Street about sixty years ago. Many of the small cottages were let to canal boat people who stayed in town for a couple of days whilst their boats were unloaded.

This aerial photograph of the centre of old Runcorn is believed to have been taken during the late 1920s. Holy Trinity Church, the public swimming baths and the police station - formerly the town hall - still remain prominent today but all the houses and industrial buildings seen to the south of Bridge Street and High Street have given way to redevelopment as have the old streets near to Holy Trinity.

A hero's grave. The grave in Runcorn Cemetery of local man Thomas ("Todger") Jones V.C., D.C.M. who won the Victoria Cross at Morval in France during World War I.

A tree-lined Main Street, Halton, in the early years of the century.

A view of High Street looking east. It is hard to believe that this was probably the busiest street in Runcorn.

The ancient market place of Halton village as it was about 1970. Sadly, the 500-year old barn to the right of the picture was demolished without the details of its unique construction being recorded for posterity.

This was the view across the fields to Halton until about 1974. Writing of this fine prospect in 1971 the famous architect Sir Nikolaus Pevsner said, "Soon it will be New Runcorn and may the planners fully realize what a visual treasure they have in this rock."

Another view of Halton Castle and village seen from Halton Brook. The photograph dates from about 1908. The fields are now occupied by the houses of the New Town.

The end of an era. For centuries the cows had been taken along Halton Main Street to the fields. This was the last occasion this would take place, for the next day, Rock Farm was taken over by the New Town developers and the cattle were sold.

The great water tower at Norton was built in 1892. It is 34 metres high and its tank holds 3,000 tons of water. Once it stood in splendid isolation but within the last ten years it has become surrounded by housing. This was the view looking down Norton Lane, Halton, about 1965.

Now but a memory. The fields of Halton have been built over to provide the Shopping City and Southgate.